HEINEMANN Profiles

Steven Spielberg

Sean Connolly

First published in Great Britain by
Heinemann Library
Halley Court, Jordan Hill,
Oxford OX2 8EJ
a division of Reed Educational and
Professional Publishing Ltd.
Heinemann is a registered trademark of Reed
Educational & Professional Publishing Limited.

OXFORD MELBOURNE AUCKLAND
KUALA LUMPUR SINGAPORE IBADAN
NAIROBI KAMPALA JOHANNESBURG
GABORONE PORTSMOUTH NH
CHICAGO

Designed by Visual Image, Taunton.
Printed in Hong Kong / China

Details of written sources:
Joseph McBride, *Steven Spielberg: A Biography*,
Simon & Schuster, 1997; Virginia Meachum,
Steven Spielberg: Hollywood Film-maker, Enslow,
1996; Donald R Mott and Cheryl McAllister
Saunders, *Steven Spielberg*, Twayne, 1996; Frank
Sanello, *Spielberg: The Man, the Movies, the
Mythology*, Taylor, 1996; David Thompson, 'Pipe
Dreams' in *Independent on Sunday* magazine, 15
June 1997, pp14–15; Andrew Yule, *Spielberg:
Father of the Man*, Warner Books, 1996.

03 02 01 00 99
10 9 8 7 6 5 4 3 2 1

ISBN 0 431 08616 8
This title is also available in a hardback library
edition (ISBN 0 431 08609 5)

**British Library Cataloguing in Publication
Data**

Connolly, Sean,
  Steven Spielberg. – (Heinemann Profiles)
  1. Spielberg, Steven, 1947– – Juvenile
  literature 2. Motion picture producers and
  directors – United States – Biography –
  Juvenile literature
  I. Title
  791.4'30233'092

Acknowledgements
The Publishers would like to thank the
following for permission to reproduce
photographs: All Action Pictures p49; Aquarius
Library pp18, 26, 28 (bottom), 30; Susan Roper
Arndt p16; BFI Stills, Posters and Designs pp20,
23, 34, 38, 44; Corbis-Bettman pp10, 40, 47, 48,
51; Pacha p4, Reuters p45; UPI p36; Ronald
Grant Archive pp25, 28 (top), 31, 39, 43;
HHPFT/Science and Society Picture Library
p12; Richard Y Hoffman Jr pp7, 9; Loretta
Knoblach p8; Kobal Collection pp14, 32, 33, 37,
41; Moviestore Collection pp22, 46; Robert
Opie p35.

Cover photograph reproduced with permission
of Rex Features.

Every effort has been made to contact copyright
holders of any material reproduced in this book.
Any omissions will be rectified in subsequent
printings if notice is given to the Publisher.

Any words appearing in the text in bold, **like
this,** are explained in the Glossary.

CONTENTS

WHO IS STEVEN SPIELBERG?

Steven Spielberg is the world's most successful film-maker. Hundreds of millions of people around the world have seen his films, which include two of the most popular films of all time: *Jurassic Park* and *E.T. : The Extraterrestrial*. It sometimes seems that everything he touches turns to gold, but Spielberg has had his share of mistakes and failures as well.

MASTER OF TECHNIQUE

Spielberg is known mainly as a **director** of films. He is able to guess how audiences will react to a scene in a film. He is skilled in making a film excite, sadden or amuse people as they watch it.

Steven Spielberg plans a shot on the set of Lost World: Jurassic Park, 1996.

This skill, particularly when it is repeated in the making of film after film, is rare, and Spielberg is greatly admired for this ability to touch the audience. Spielberg's films communicate a child-like wonder about the world around him.

Personal reflections

Spielberg understands **suburban life,** television and fast cars, all of which became more common in his childhood in 1950s America. Films such as *Jaws* and *Close Encounters of the Third Kind* succeed because they are about ordinary people, even though they are involved in extraordinary events.

As his career has developed, however, Spielberg has been able to touch on even deeper aspects of his past. As a child, Spielberg's Jewish background exposed him to the darker side of human nature. Other children often treated him as an 'outsider' and he was the only Jewish child at his school. Touching on this experience, he went on to direct *Schindler's List*, his masterful account of the **persecution** of the Jews during the Second World War.

'Directing is 80 per cent communicating and 20 per cent know-how.'
Steven Spielberg, 1987

Just how did this young director from the American suburbs become such a success?

CHILD OF THE SUBURBS

Steven Allan Spielberg, the eldest child of Arnold and Leah Spielberg, was born in Cincinnati, Ohio, on 18 December 1946. The Spielbergs were Jewish and Steven's first memories – when he was only six months old – were of being wheeled in a pram down the aisles of the local **synagogue**, with bearded men appearing as shadows against a bright light. Steven's awareness of his Jewish heritage would play an important part in his life.

In different ways, each of Steven's parents would also have a deep influence on the young boy's upbringing and character. Arnold was an electrical engineer and was interested in computers, which had only just been developed at the time of Steven's birth. Leah, on the other hand, was the artistic parent. She had given up a promising career as a concert pianist when she married and settled down.

The Spielbergs' other children were all girls – Anne, Sue and Nancy. As the four children grew older, they would become playmates, finding fun in each other's company each time the family settled in a new neighbourhood. Arnold's job meant they often had to move to different parts of the country. The first move in 1949 took the Spielbergs to Haddonfield, New Jersey. The journey took them from America's Middle West to the bustling East Coast.

In his early teens Steven became a Boy Scout, enjoying the companionship and teamwork that came from Scouting activities.

When Steven was six, his father took him to Philadelphia to see his first film, *The Greatest Show on Earth*. Steven enjoyed this exciting circus story, but a few things puzzled him about this new experience. At first he could not understand how a circus could perform on a flat screen, and part of him felt disappointed that he couldn't smell the sawdust and gunpowder.

The Spielbergs' house in New Jersey, like millions of suburban homes across the United States, was built in the years immediately following the Second World War.

In 1954 the family moved again, this time to Scottsdale, Arizona, a **suburb** of Phoenix in the desert country of the American Southwest. Steven, who was already showing signs of being a sensitive child, was upset by the move, although his mother assured him of the exciting times that lay ahead.

Being a stranger in a new school was also difficult. Steven was a slow reader and not very good at the games the other children played. Once, he and 50 of his schoolmates set off on a mile run. After a while all the runners had completed the course, except for Steven and John, a mentally handicapped boy. The other children cheered John on and Steven deliberately slowed his own pace so that the other boy would cross the finishing line first. The crowd carried John away on their shoulders while Steven remained on the track crying.

Steven was not good at games, but this was not the only reason for his feelings of isolation. He was the only Jewish child at school, and some of the other children made spiteful remarks about this. The worst came when a group of schoolchildren gathered in front of the house and shouted: 'The Spielbergs are dirty Jews! The Spielbergs are dirty Jews!'

Arnold Spielberg accompanied Steven (centre) and other Boy Scouts on trips into the Arizona mountains.

HOME MOVIES

Scottsdale was in many ways a typical American suburb in the 1950s. People lived in detached houses, looked after small gardens, played ball and had barbecues. Children would go to each other's houses to play, or ride their bikes around the neighbourhood.

Steven's own sensitive character, coupled with the teasing that he often received at school, meant that for him none of these 'normal' activities was very exciting.

Television was still a novelty in the 1950s and the whole family would sit and watch.

Instead he made his own entertainment, often at the expense of his younger sisters. He convinced them that he had a dead Second World War pilot rotting away in his bedroom and he dared them to go and have a look. When it was dark he took them into his room quietly, opened his cupboard door and shone his torch on a plastic skull wearing a helmet. Steven, the master showman, loved his success as his sisters ran off screaming.

Some early influences

As a child in the 1950s Steven Spielberg was influenced by watching films and television. His parents took him to the cinema to see action films such as *Davy Crockett* and the Walt Disney classics *Bambi*, *Fantasia* and *Snow White*. Just as important, though, were the many hours he spent watching television. Steven's parents insisted that he watch only children's programmes such as *The Mickey Mouse Club* and *The Atomic Club*. When they went out Steven would sneak down to watch some of the 'forbidden' grown-up programmes. These included exciting police shows (*Dragnet* and *Highway Patrol*), comedies (*The Honeymooners* and *Soupy Sales*) and eerie fantasy programmes (*Science Fiction Theater*).

When Steven was about seven years old, he developed a taste for television, despite the attempts his parents made to control the children's viewing. When his parents were out, Steven would wait until the baby-sitter had fallen asleep and then creep downstairs to watch television. But first, he had to deal with the 'booby trap' that his father had laid – a secretly placed hair on the television 'On' switch. Steven would memorize the position of the hair and always replace it exactly where he had found it after watching hours of police dramas, comedies and old films.

The Kodak 8mm movie camera was portable enough to take anywhere.

Eventually a chance came for Steven to combine his mischievous ability to entertain with his love of television. When Steven was twelve, Leah Spielberg gave her husband an 8mm Kodak movie camera for Father's Day. Arnold's first efforts were terrible – the images wobbled and were usually out of **focus**. Irritated by his son's constant teasing and criticism, Arnold handed Steven the camera and said 'why don't you try?'

Steven proved to be a natural with the camera. He used his toys as 'characters' and began making small adventure films. By his teens Steven had made his first short film, called *The Great Train Crash*, in which he had used his own model railway. Steven's parents were amazed by how life-like this 'disaster' appeared. They might not have realized it but Steven was also mastering important film techniques such as **continuity** and **composition**.

DEVELOPING A GIFT

Before long the Spielberg house began to look like a film set, with furniture and lights constantly being moved around to prepare for a new film. Steven was not shy about using his sisters' toys in some of his productions; even today they must have mixed feelings about *The Terror of the Burning Doll's House*.

The movie camera was Steven's constant companion. He filmed the family at home and on holiday, particularly during their hiking trips in the Arizona countryside. Steven constantly worked on his self-taught technique, but his early efforts show how much he was helped by his parents' influence. His vivid imagination and choice of subject matter reflected his mother's artistic nature, but Steven's emphasis on accuracy and precision came from his father.

A Taste of Success

'Mom, we're shooting tomorrow,' Steven would say, and that would be enough for his mother to abandon plans to have friends round for coffee or to practise her own music. By the time Steven had reached his early teens the Spielberg house looked more and more like a miniature film **studio**. Floodlights, strung together with thick electric cables, shone down on the family rooms. Mountains made of papier-mâché acted as backdrops for the scenes being played. And overseeing it all was Steven, camera held to the eye, always on the lookout for the best shot.

Film-making had become Steven's life, and he spent the summer holidays doing odd jobs for neighbours in order to earn money for new equipment. He even rented films and projected them at home, with his mother and sisters selling popcorn and soft drinks to his schoolmate 'customers'.

School became better for Steven now that he had such fun at home. He began shooting films with actors and even used his film-making skills to stop some of the bullying that he got at school. One boy, who had previously made life difficult for Steven, became the star of a forty-minute war film, *Battle Squad*. The boy enjoyed it and became a good friend.

A PERSONAL TOUR

Hollywood, with its busy film studios, remained Steven's dream. He was able to follow that dream in 1963 during a summer holiday in California with his cousins. Like thousands of other tourists, Steven bought a ticket for the guided tour of Universal Studios. But as everyone else boarded the tour bus he hid, and then set about exploring on his own. He wandered on to sets and even met the famous **director** John Ford. One film editor was so impressed with the young visitor that he handed him a one-day pass. Steven waved the pass at guards and decided to do the same thing every day for the rest of the summer.

American Artist Productions

PRESENTS

World Première
OF THE MOTION PICTURE

FIRELIGHT

Phoenix Little Theatre

March 24, 1964
8:00 P.M.

Special programmes were printed for Firelight, Steven Spielberg's first real film, which showed a confidence and skill far beyond his years.

Steven hoped that the film world would be impressed with the short films that he packed in his briefcase but the reaction at Universal was only luke-warm. Still, the film bug had definitely bitten, and when Steven returned to Arizona he borrowed $400 from his father and set about making a **feature-length** film.

The new project was a science fiction film called *Firelight*, a tale about UFOs that attack Earth. Although Steven was only 16 years old, he persuaded student actors from Arizona State University to act in the film. He even managed to get the local airport to close down a runway for one scene. The length was as ambitious as the plot, and the finished film ran to 140 minutes.

Arnold Spielberg hired the local Scottsdale cinema for one night, and *Firelight* had its 'world premiere' on 24 March 1964. When Steven examined the **box-office** takings, they showed that the public had spent $500 on tickets. The film had cleared a $100 profit.

Steven was lucky to have met the sometimes cranky John Ford when the **director** was in a sunny mood. Ford even gave Steven some practical tips about film-making, which ended with the most important advice, 'Never use your own money to make a movie.'

A Helping Hand

Steven did not have much time to savour the one-night success of *Firelight*. The next day the family moved to Saratoga, a suburb of San Jose in northern California. Yet again Steven had to settle into a new school. At Los Gatos High School he had no friends, and he had to put up with vicious **anti-Semitic** comments in the halls of the school. There were constant threats of violence, so for the last six months of his time at school, Steven was picked up by his parents at the end of each day.

Because Steven's grades at school had only been average he could not attend the university of his choice. He wanted to enrol at the prestigious film school of the University of California at Los Angeles.

Spielberg enrolled at California State University in 1965, but his studies were cut short by his film ambitions.

CAMPUS EVENTS

ate Orientation Program
8:30 AM   Sep 6
or info Call 985-5515

CALIFORNIA STATE UNIVERSITY
LONG BEACH

Instead, he chose to study English at California State University at Long Beach. At least this choice of university would bring him physically closer to **Hollywood**.

BACK TO THE STUDIO

While Steven was a student he began spending three days a week back at Universal Studios. Again he watched masters at work, and once more he tried to impress the film people. His determined attitude and enthusiasm finally paid off when he met a young man named Denis Hoffman, who ran a company that produced **special effects** for films. Hoffman offered Spielberg the chance to direct a short film, called *Amblin'*, about a boy and girl who meet in the California desert and hitchhike to the Pacific Ocean.

The film had no words, but used a **soundtrack** performed by musicians who had business links with Hoffman. *Amblin'* was completed in the late summer of 1968 when Steven was just 21 years old. The **negative** of the 24-minute film was stored in a laboratory at Universal Studios. It would prove to be a lucky omen for Steven, because *Amblin'* was going to be 'third time lucky' in his dealings with the great **studio**.

IN AT THE DEEP END

After all the years Steven Spielberg had spent dreaming about getting into **Hollywood**, his breakthrough came almost in an instant. Chuck Silvers, a Universal Studios editor who had met Spielberg, persuaded Sidney J Sheinberg, president of Universal's television department, to watch *Amblin'*. Sheinberg was impressed and arranged a meeting with Spielberg. He was convinced that Spielberg had the talent to become an accomplished **director** and he offered him a seven-year contract. Spielberg decided to give up his studies and take the deal, which was signed within a week.

Still in his early 20s, Spielberg (left) had to direct Hollywood stars such as Joan Crawford.

THE YOUNG PROFESSIONAL

At just 22 years old, Steven Spielberg was given his first professional assignment – to direct an episode from the television series *Night Gallery*. In keeping with the spooky nature of the series, the plot was about a wealthy, but blind woman, who pays a fortune to be able to see for a short time. The sting in the tail comes when there is an electrical blackout just as she regains her sight.

Spielberg relished the challenge and used many of the directing techniques that he had learned or developed over the years. But this was the first time that he had to direct professional actors, and one of the stars was Joan Crawford, once one of the leading lights in Hollywood. There were delays in shooting and afterwards Spielberg was disappointed to learn that much of the episode had been reworked to get rid of his 'fancy' techniques.

Despite the bumpy start, Spielberg soon learned to provide what the television executives were expecting. He did more work on *Night Gallery* as well as on other series. One of his favourites was 'LA–2017', an episode of the series *Name of the Game*. The episode, in which the star is hit on the head and wakes up in the 21st century, gave Spielberg the chance to indulge his love of science fiction.

Amblin' to success

Just as Spielberg's television career was beginning to take off he got another boost. *Amblin'* was entered in various film festivals and won the Silver Phoenix Award at the 1969 Atlanta Film Festival. Years later Spielberg recognized the importance of this short film when he set up his own production company, naming it Amblin Entertainment.

BREAKING FREE

While working for Universal, Spielberg found that television put many limits on the type of ideas he wanted to explore, both in subject and technique. He began to worry about losing the enthusiasm that had taken him so far. Could he find a way round this problem?

The answer came with the TV movie *Duel*. Spielberg read the **screenplay** and convinced Universal executives that he could tell the story of a man terrorized on the open road by a huge lorry. The man – and the audience – never see the driver of the lorry, which adds to the suspense. Spielberg used some of the techniques that were discouraged in the other television programmes. He also used tricks from the famous 'Road Runner' cartoons. Just as the driver thinks he has outrun the lorry, it appears once more, ready to attack. The suspense builds throughout the film until the lorry finally plunges over a cliff and bursts into flames.

Dennis Weaver, the star of Duel, portrayed an 'ordinary guy' – a type of hero that would appear in later Spielberg films.

The sprawling expanse of Universal Studios is as large as a small town.

Duel was broadcast on ABC Television in the USA in 1971, and proved to be one of the most popular TV movies ever shown. Universal bought the film back from ABC, got Spielberg to film new sequences, and then distributed it to cinemas outside the United States. Spielberg travelled to Europe to help **promote** *Duel* and to accept an award from a film festival in Sicily. He made a special trip to Rome to meet Federico Fellini, the great Italian film **director** whose name alone was enough to sell his films.

American TV

Steven Spielberg was fortunate to perfect his film-making skills at a time when each episode of some popular American television programmes told its own story, much like a film itself. These were good experience for the young director. As well as *Night Gallery* and *Name of the Game*, Spielberg directed episodes of *Marcus Welby, MD*, *Owen Marshall*, *Counselor at Law* and he even directed the first episode of the extremely popular detective series *Columbo*, starring Peter Falk.

NOW FOR THE BIG SCREEN

With the success of *Duel*, both on television and in international cinemas, Spielberg had shown that he could carry a full-length film all the way from the planning stage to the finished product. And for the big **Hollywood studios**, the most important thing was that the finished product made a good profit. Now Spielberg's job was to make the big move into films that were planned for cinema release in the first place.

Spielberg set about the task with patience and determination. He was offered the chance to direct *White Lightning*, a thriller starring one of Hollywood's most popular actors, Burt Reynolds. Spielberg spent three months preparing for this job, looking at **locations** and agreeing on a **cast**. Later, he decided that the film was never going to be anything special, and it might stop his career just as it was starting, so he chose to drop the project.

AMERICA ON WHEELS

Finally, Spielberg convinced Universal to let him film *The Sugarland Express*, which was based on the true story of a Texan woman and her escaped convict husband who try to regain **custody** of their baby. The film was extremely difficult to make, largely because most of the plot centred on a thrilling car chase across Texas.

William Atherton (left) and Goldie Hawn play the runaway couple who kidnap a policeman in *The Sugarland Express* (1974).

The 'express' of the title is the ever-growing line of cars following the fugitives, including police cars, news reporters and excitement-seeking onlookers.

Sugarland Express proved to be an exciting film, with twists in the plot mirroring the twists, turns and flips of the speeding cars. Unfortunately, two similar films had recently appeared on American cinema screens, so its success was limited. Spielberg had another reason for the film's relatively poor performance – he tried to tell too many stories at once and the plot got confused. In his next film he would tell one big story without being side-tracked.

And what a story it turned out to be.

Although *Sugarland Express* was not a full commercial success, it caught the eye of many film critics. One of these critics, Pauline Kael of the influential *New Yorker* magazine, even said: 'In terms of the pleasure that technical assurance gives an audience, *Sugarland* is one of the most phenomenal debuts in the history of movies.'

SHARK ATTACK!

Even before *The Sugarland Express* had been released, Steven Spielberg had lined up his next project. In the summer of 1973 he read the **galley proofs** of *Jaws*, a novel that was about to be published. Spielberg was fascinated by this tale of a coastal town being terrorized by a great white shark, and he decided that he would like to direct it. 'I wanted to do *Jaws* for hostile reasons,' he said later. 'I read it and felt that I had been attacked.'

The successful **Hollywood producers** Richard D Zanuck and David Brown owned the **film rights** to the novel *Jaws* and Spielberg used all his powers of persuasion to convince them to let him direct the film version. They finally agreed, and the film went into the planning stage with Spielberg at the helm.

The beach scenes in Jaws (1975) captured the sense of the swimmers' panic when they learn that a killer shark is just offshore.

Spielberg had clear ideas about how the novel should be made into a film. He wanted to concentrate on the basic conflict between the ordinary people and the brute force of nature, so he cut some of the less exciting 'dry land' parts out of the screen version. Then, after spending many hours watching *20,000 Leagues Under the Sea*, *Moby Dick* and other 'sea' films, Spielberg decided that *Jaws* must be filmed on **location**, without using **studio** water tanks to mimic the look of the sea.

The technical crew chose Martha's Vineyard, an island off the coast of Massachusetts, as the ideal location. The island was big enough to accommodate a large film crew and it had water at least 10.5 metres deep, with a flat sandy bottom.

Filming began in the summer of 1974. What neither Spielberg nor his crew had anticipated were the crowds of holidaymakers and the hundreds of small boats that seemed to be drifting into every scene. Also, the weather was changeable – a constant problem for **continuity** – and treacherous currents could sweep away expensive equipment or even one of the stars. In fact, they lost two cameras and Spielberg himself was once swept overboard.

The young **director** had to keep a firm grip on every aspect of the filming schedule. He kept a close eye on the **cast**, making sure they were comfortable and happy, and tried to limit the number of sightseers who showed up each day on the set. Most importantly, Spielberg mastered the difficult controls of 'Bruce', the seven metre mechanical shark, saying it was 'about as easy to operate as a 747'.

Despite Spielberg's planning and skill, the film began to fall behind schedule. Luckily for Spielberg, he was able to rely on storyboarding to help keep the last third of the filming schedule under control. He did not leave the island until the last scene was shot, 155 days after he had arrived.

An intricate system of levers and pulleys operated 'Bruce', the mechanical Jaws (1975).

Storyboarding

Storyboarding, which Spielberg used to keep a grip on the production of *Jaws*, is a method of planning the way in which a film is shot. The director breaks down the script into a number of detailed pictures, each of which represents 'the ideal frame' of a particular scene. The director can indicate other things on the storyboard, such as where to point the cameras and how the actors should move within this frame. By solving many problems before shooting begins, storyboarding can save time – and money – later on in the schedule.

'For years he just scared us. Now he gets to scare the masses.'
    Anne, Spielberg's sister, after seeing *Jaws*, 1975

'My next picture will be on dry land. There won't even be a bathroom scene.'   Spielberg, 1975, acknowledging the difficulties of filming near the sea

The finished version of *Jaws* opened in American cinemas in the spring of 1975. The public loved it. The film earned $7 million in its first three days of release and went on to earn over $260 million in American cinemas alone. This broke all existing records, and the 28-year-old director leapfrogged to the forefront of the film world.

What's the Big Idea?

Hollywood studios usually take great care before committing themselves to the expense of a new feature film. They usually look for films with a 'big idea', that is, an easily understood concept that drives the plot and holds the audience's attention from start to finish. *Jaws* passes the 'big idea' test easily because its central theme of a man-eating shark terrorizing a holiday resort takes hold and never lets go – rather like a shark bite!

Look to the Skies

The record-breaking success of *Jaws* gave Steven Spielberg a great deal of power and influence within **Hollywood**. In particular, it meant that he could follow his own ideas for films, knowing that he would almost certainly be able to direct the film of his own choice. For his next film he looked upward as well as to his own past.

Developing the idea

Spielberg's first long film, *Firelight*, made when he was only sixteen, developed one of his favourite themes – intelligent life in outer space. While he was making *Jaws*, he developed a story about Unidentified Flying Objects (UFOs). This first idea was entitled 'Watch the Skies' and concerned a US Air Force officer who had to help the government pretend that there were no such things as UFOs. Columbia Pictures agreed to the idea, and Spielberg asked the screenwriters from *The Sugarland Express* to write the script, which became *Close Encounters of the Third Kind*.

Filming Close Encounters (1977) allowed Spielberg to work with one of his own heroes, the French film director Francois Truffaut (centre).

A Columbia/EMI Presentation
THE SPECIAL EDITION
CLOSE ENCOUNTERS OF THE THIRD KIND A

The story is based around a group of ordinary people who find themselves drawn to a mysterious mountain in the American West. Once they reach it they find a group of people waiting for a huge spaceship to land. The spaceship makes contact with them and once it lands, aliens come out to welcome the humans on board, to go with them into space. The characters, like the audience, have no idea what to expect when they reach the spacecraft but they are driven by unstoppable curiosity.

Publicity posters for Close Encounters captured the film's sense of awe and mystery.

ANOTHER HIT

Close Encounters of the Third Kind was a gamble for Spielberg and Columbia, and its first reviews were negative. However, the cinema-going public provided Spielberg with another **box-office** hit, increasing his power and influence within Hollywood. It seemed that Spielberg could not fail – or could he?

Spielberg and the Oscars

Steven Spielberg was nominated for the Best Director Academy Award for *Close Encounters*. These awards, are the American film industry's highest praise. Spielberg failed to win the **Oscar,** just as he had when *Jaws* had failed in its nomination for Best Picture. Many people wondered whether Hollywood was jealous of his success.

FAILURE AND SUCCESS

Spielberg's films had always relied on the humour in everyday details, and so it was not surprising that he thought he could direct a comedy. In 1978 he set about making *1941*, a non-stop action comedy set in Los Angeles during the Second World War. This project, however, only showed Spielberg's limitations. He hired many of America's most popular comedians in the hope that their presence alone would make the film funny.

Spielberg, seen here with Robert Stack and Toshiro Mifune, tried hard to create a comic atmosphere in *1941*.

The mix of constant explosions, plane crashes and chaotic running around failed to find America's funny bone. Although *1941* made some money worldwide during its 1979 release, most people viewed it as a failure, although they might not have gone so far as the *Washington Post*, which described it as 'an appalling waste of film-making'.

BACK WITH A VENGEANCE

Upset and tired by the whole ordeal of *1941*, Spielberg gratefully accepted an offer of a holiday in Hawaii with his friend George Lucas, the **director** of *Star Wars*. There they came up with the story that would become *Raiders of the Lost Ark*.

Spielberg's good working relationship with Harrison Ford helped turn Raiders of the Lost Ark into box-office gold (1981).

Spielberg and Lucas were looking back to the same era as the events of *1941*, but they stayed within territory that they knew how to handle. They created the American hero Indiana Jones who single-handedly takes on what seems to be half of Nazi Germany and outwits them. The film and the hero are based on cinema **serials** of the 1930s and 1940s, with the plot building with a series of cliff-hanging adventures. Spielberg directed the film with just the right touch of humour and pace, and the finished product turned out to be the most successful American film of 1981.

Aged 34, Spielberg was back where he felt happiest, able to work on his favourite projects.

Feelings of doubt

Spielberg had his doubts about whether *1941* would be a success, or even funny. Typically using a **Hollywood** comparison (from the film *The Wizard of Oz)* he admitted in 1978: 'Yes. I'm scared. I'm like the Cowardly Lion, and two smashes back to back have not strengthened my belief in my ability to deliver.'

TRIUMPH AND TRAGEDY

How much is the name 'Steven Spielberg' worth when it appears above a film's title? By the early 1980s the answer was millions, even hundreds of millions. Spielberg had wealth, power and most importantly, creative freedom to choose or develop film ideas. Sometimes he might be too busy to direct one of these films, but his involvement – and more importantly, his credit as **executive producer** – would sell the film.

E.T. was a complicated mixture of mechanics, electronics and actors, including a mime artist and two dwarves.

It was in these circumstances that Spielberg became involved with the film *Poltergeist*. The idea for this story about poltergeists, playful ghosts, was Spielberg's, and he claimed to have written the **screenplay** in five days. The film was directed by Tobe Hooper and showed all the signs of a Spielberg film, as it was about ordinary people coping with extraordinary events. The success of *Poltergeist*, however, was nothing like Spielberg's next project as **director**, which became the film phenomenon of the 1980s.

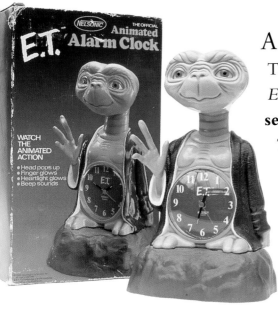

A CLOSER ENCOUNTER

The heart-warming film *E.T.: The Extraterrestrial* began as a possible **sequel** to *Close Encounters of the Third Kind*. Spielberg had asked screenwriter John Sayles to produce a screenplay that would recapture the sense of wonder of *Close Encounters of the Third Kind*. One of Sayles's main ideas was that an alien might be left behind by a departing spacecraft. The resulting story of how E.T. is befriended by Elliot, and later by his brother and sister, works like a fairy tale.

The film E.T. gave birth to products which earned $1 billion worldwide.

In directing this film, Spielberg left behind his storyboarding technique. This gave him more scope to make changes to the filming plans on the spur of the moment. He put more of himself into the film, remembering ideas that he had had since he was a child.

Audiences clearly shared these feelings of wonder and the industry recognized Spielberg's ability to touch viewers as much as the greatest 'family' directors before him. One critic summed this up by describing *E.T.* as 'the best Disney film that Walt Disney never made.'

'I feel I'm still a kid. I'm 35 and I haven't really grown up yet.'
Steven Spielberg, 1982, the year of *E.T.*

A SUDDEN SHOCK

A crew of mechanics examine the wreck of the helicopter that killed three actors on the set of Twilight Zone.

On 23 July 1982, just two weeks after the triumphant opening of *E.T.*, Steven Spielberg received some devastating news. Three actors, including two children, had been killed on the set of *Twilight Zone*, a film that Spielberg was producing. A helicopter had gone out of control and crashed into the three actors. To make matters worse, the two children had been hired without permits. It was the law to have permits, which set out guidelines on working conditions for child film actors.

Twilight Zone was made up of four parts, each with a different director. Spielberg himself was directing one of the stories but the accident happened in the part directed by John Landis. A series of investigations and a legal trial followed. Landis and other crew members were eventually found not guilty of involuntary **manslaughter** in 1987.

Although neither Spielberg nor Warner Brothers faced any charges, the events of the tragedy lived on to haunt Spielberg. Could he move forward if he dwelt endlessly on *Twilight Zone* and its effects?

Full circle

The *Twilight Zone* project meant more to Spielberg than some of the other films he produced. It was a tribute to Rod Serling, a talented screenwriter of the 1950s and 1960s who presented a spooky television series of the same name. The Serling connection was a strong one for Spielberg – it was Serling who wrote *Night Gallery*, the first television job that Spielberg had completed back in 1969.

WEARING TWO HATS AGAIN

A fter the *Twilight Zone* tragedy Spielberg went back to his known strengths – directing action blockbusters and making films that reflected his own views of life. During 1983 he directed a second Indiana Jones film, *Indiana Jones and the Temple of Doom*, and produced a film called *Gremlins*.

TURNING THE TABLES

The Temple of Doom, described as a **prequel** to *Raiders of the Lost Ark*, received lots of publicity. But it was almost overshadowed by the second project. *Gremlins* concerned mischievous creatures that reminded audiences of *E.T.*, but the similarity soon ends. Cuddly and sweet at first, the gremlins change character when they are exposed to water.

The public loved watching a typical American small town descend into chaos as the creatures run riot. Eventually calm is restored and the original gremlin is returned to the wise old Chinese storekeeper who first looked after it. The story ends with the old man explaining that 'society without responsibility is society without hope'.

Director Joe Dante (right) welcomed Spielberg's comments and advice on the set of Gremlins in 1983.

  PG
and the
TEMPLE OF DOOM

TM & © 1984 LUCASFILM LTD.

One exciting scene in Indiana Jones and the Temple of Doom sent its stars Harrison Ford and Kate Capshaw, hurtling down a mine shaft.

OVERDOING IT?

Indiana Jones and the Temple of Doom saw one of cinema's favourite heroes battling his way through adventures in China, Thailand and India. Like _Raiders of the Lost Ark_, _The Temple of Doom_ was an enormous commercial success.

The new film, however, was criticized for the use of violence and the way in which it seemed to show Asian people as shifty or evil. Spielberg was hurt by these criticisms. He tried to play down his involvement in the film, describing himself as a 'hired hand'. He admitted that he would not allow a ten-year-old to see the film: 'The responsibility to the children of this country is worth any loss at the **box-office**.'

Perhaps the 'child' in him was beginning to grow up. But would it show in any of his next films?

New Horizons

Spielberg was at a crossroads by the mid-1980s. He wanted to be taken seriously by critics as someone who could deal with mature, adult issues. Perhaps success in that area would lead to an **Oscar**.

A NEW FAMILY

At this time Spielberg's personal life changed. In the early stages of his career he had thrown himself into his work, turning down invitations to parties and other social events, especially while making a film. But in 1985 he married the actress Amy Irving. A son, Max Samuel, was born that same year. Spielberg's choice of films also began to change. He directed *The Color Purple*, about a group of African-American women and the difficulties they face. The film was quite successful, but the critics insisted that Spielberg had toned down the original novel in order to make a **mainstream** film.

Spielberg and his wife Amy Irving attended many formal functions in Hollywood.

RISKS AND SECURITY

Because *The Color Purple* was successful, despite the critical reaction, it was felt that Spielberg could handle material that **Hollywood** considered risky. In 1986 Spielberg took on another 'risky' project, a film version of the novel *Empire of the Sun*.

Spielberg took great care to get just the right performances from Whoopi Goldberg and other cast members of The Color Purple (1985).

The book, by British novelist JG Ballard, looks at the outbreak of the Second World War through the eyes of a young English boy who is living in China. Spielberg uses the study of human nature, rather than chases and explosions, to hold the audience's interest. The film received mixed reviews, with Spielberg fans hating the film and Spielberg critics praising it.

Spielberg returned to familiar ground for the third part of the Indiana Jones **trilogy**, *Indiana Jones and the Last Crusade*, made in 1989. Even the familiar 'Indy antics' were given a new, more mature, slant and much of the film's success came from the lively exchanges between Indy and his father, played by veteran star Sean Connery.

'He gets physically ill when a project is over. The people involved become his family. He loves them and hates for it to be done and to leave everyone.'
Anne Spielberg, sister

Towering Achievements

Spielberg's marriage to Amy Irving did not stand up to the strains of the couple's ambitious **Hollywood** lives. They divorced in April 1989. In October 1991 Spielberg married Kate Capshaw, who had starred in *Indiana Jones and the Temple of Doom*. At around the same time Spielberg released *Hook*, a version of JM Barrie's much-loved book *Peter Pan*. The film failed miserably, leaving Spielberg unable to make his mark on the new decade.

The roots of success

Few could have known that Spielberg would be able to do just that with his next two films, which were hugely successful, and finally received the highest critical praise.

In 1982 Spielberg had come across the novel *Schindler's Ark*. The novel tells the true story of Oskar Schindler, a German businessman who saved the lives of Jewish workers and rescued others from Nazi death camps during the Second World War. Remembering his own Jewish background, Spielberg became sure that the novel should be filmed. But who would direct such a powerful story?

Directing dinosaurs

That problem nagged Spielberg throughout the 1980s, but by the early 1990s he was certain that he

could do the job, backed up by his production company, Amblin Entertainment. Spielberg showed the idea to Universal Studios, and they agreed – as long as he would direct one of their projects first.

That 'project' turned out to be *Jurassic Park*, the action-filled story of a dinosaur theme park where the animals break free. Spielberg and his crew did much of the shooting on the Hawaiian island of Kauai. Just as shooting was beginning, a fierce hurricane swept across the island, killing 3 people and leaving 8000 homeless.

The film did go on once the rubble was cleared and finally the **location** shooting was completed. The only problem was that there were no dinosaurs at this stage – they were to be added using high-tech **special effects**.

Exploring his soul

By now Spielberg had flown to Poland to work on *Schindler's List*. By day he shot scenes from the new film and in the evening he oversaw the **special effects** of *Jurassic Park*, which were sent via satellite from the United States. Spielberg's devotion to *Schindler's List* made it a masterpiece full of excellent direction and fine performances from its **cast**.

He shot the film in black and white, to add to the feel that it was a document recording the events of the **Holocaust**. He remembered stories from his mother and grandfather as he filmed the tragic events of that brutal time. Slowly the film began to reveal itself as a personal, deeply felt statement.

Spielberg personally chose actor Liam Neeson to play the lead role in Schindler's List (1993).

'I mustn't use my Spielbergian bag of tricks here. I must simply eavesdrop with the camera, just tell the story, keep peeling that onion away, get very, very bare and stark.'
Spielberg on his technique for *Schindler's List*

REAPING THE REWARDS

Spielberg proudly holds two of the 1994 Oscars won by Schindler's List, flanked by his mother and his wife, Kate Capshaw.

Both films were released in 1993. *Jurassic Park* swept aside the previous record–breaking money earner, *E.T.*, and earned nearly $1 billion worldwide. Spielberg received about $40 million for his direction and earned even more from the many products that used the 'Jurassic Park' name.

Spielberg earned less from *Schindler's List*, although that hardly mattered because the film became an instant classic. There was almost universal praise for one of the best films ever made. The icing on the cake came during the next Academy Awards ceremony, when *Schindler's List* won seven **Oscars**, including Best **Director** for Spielberg.

'It should be noted … that Mr Spielberg has this year delivered the most astounding one-two punch in the history of American cinema.'
New York Times film critic Janet Maslin, 1993

Counting his Blessings

For several years after *Schindler's List* and *Jurassic Park* Spielberg took a break from directing. In many ways he had finally proved himself to audiences, critics and most importantly, to himself. He still worked on other films through his production company, Amblin Entertainment.

One good turn deserves another

Spielberg also had the chance to offer someone else some of the success and lucky breaks he felt he had received. As **producer** of the film *Casper*, based on the cartoon series about a friendly ghost, Spielberg offered 30-year-old Brad Silberling a big break, just as Universal's Sid Sheinberg had done for him. Silberling had wanted to become a **director** after first seeing *Jaws*. Like Spielberg he had spent years with a home movie camera before getting a job in television. Spielberg liked what he saw.

Jeff Goldblum (left) was one of the Jurassic Park stars who returned in Lost World: Jurassic Park, (1997).

Spielberg has helped raise millions for the Survivors of the Shoah Visual History Foundation.

He offered him the director's job and provided moral support while the film was being made. The film went on to earn more than $100 million, leaving everyone happy with Spielberg's choice of director.

Two views of the past

Spielberg found the ideal '**sequel**' to *Schindler's List*. He gave the millions of dollars he earned from the film to the Survivors of the Shoah Visual History Foundation, a non-profit organization devoted to recording the story of **Holocaust** victims and their families. Spielberg also helped to attract money from big business.

'I cry every time I get involved in watching someone's story. But I don't turn away. If I do, what can I expect others to do?'

Spielberg on his work with the Survivors of the Shoah Visual History Foundation, 1994

The sequel to *Jurassic Park* was more commercial. In 1997 Spielberg directed and released *Lost World: Jurassic Park*. Although **box-office** sales did not reach the astronomical heights of the first film, it swept the world on its release.

Still Dreaming of Success

Steven Spielberg had long remembered the words of the veteran film **director** John Ford: 'Never use your own money to make a movie'. That advice had seemed sound during the years when Spielberg was a relatively unknown director and no one was sure that his films would make a profit. He earned a fee for each film, which increased as a percentage of the film's earnings as he became more successful. But the largest share of the profits went to the **studio**.

Hollywood's newest studio

With this in mind, Spielberg and two business colleagues, Jeffrey Katzenberg and David Geffen, decided to set up their own studio. DreamWorks SKG was formed on 11 October 1994, and its aims are to make films, television programmes and records.

Spielberg relaxes with Dream Works SKG partners Jeffrey Katzenberg and David Geffen.

The team of founders knows that Spielberg's name sells films, but they also know that big gambles can lead to equally big losses. No one knows this risk more than Spielberg himself. Another such risk is his 1998 film *Amistad*, which is about a slave **revolt** in the 1800s.

Spielberg the family man enjoys time at home as much as making films.

A GROWING FAMILY

As well as having a new team at work, Spielberg has a growing 'team' at home – his wife and children. His family now includes seven children – two from his marriage to Kate Capshaw, one from Capshaw's previous marriage, one from Spielberg's marriage to Amy Irving and three adopted children. The family grew particularly during the three-year break Spielberg took from directing after *Jurassic Park* and *Schindler's List*. With such company and support at home, it seems likely that Spielberg will be able to explore his theme of child-like wonder for many years to come.

'I'd like to be able to tell my child that it's all like it is in the movies. That we always slay our dragons, wake up from our nightmares, and that it's easy to tell the good guys from the bad guys.'   Steven Spielberg, 1997

The Changing View of Steven Spielberg

From the start of Steven Spielberg's career, he was praised as a skilful technical **director**. This meant that he knew how to shoot or edit a scene in order to get the audience to shriek, gasp or sigh in relief. *Jaws* made people scream, *E.T.* brought tears to the eyes and *Jurassic Park* made audiences gasp in amazement. But did this increasingly successful film-maker have anything more to offer?

Victim of his own success

Even some of Spielberg's closest colleagues felt that he was more of a commercial director than one with any particular artistic skill or depth. Sid Sheinberg, who had 'discovered' the young Spielberg and who bought the **film rights** to *Schindler's List*, considered Spielberg a 'popcorn' director without the necessary intelligence to direct that terrible tale of Nazi horror.

Such a view was common, and for many years Spielberg seemed to be like a bright child who needs the approval of the grown-ups around him. For Spielberg, the 'grown-ups' are the film critics, who in many ways are the judges of a director's reputation.

Growing up in public

Since the 1980s Spielberg has tried to explore new themes and, sometimes, failed in his attempts.

Steven Spielberg cut the ribbon at the grand opening of the Universal Studios Florida theme park in June 1990.

Some critics praised Spielberg, listing *The Color Purple*, *Empire of the Sun* and even *Always*, a romantic comedy, for their growing understanding of human nature.

With *Schindler's List*, this process was completed. Having set off on his film journey by showing the 'ordinary person' in difficult circumstances, Spielberg showed that he could explore the very nature of humanity itself.

Stanley Kauffman, of the influential *New Republic* magazine, summed up Spielberg's remarkable career in 1993: 'Spielberg has done the best directing of his career. Much of his previous work has been clever, but *Schindler's List* is masterly…a welcome astonishment from a director who has given us much boyish **esprit**, much **ingenuity**, but little seriousness. His stark, intelligent style here perfectly controlled, suggests that this may be the start of a new period in Spielberg's **prodigious** career – Part Two: the Man.'

THE FILMS OF STEVEN SPIELBERG

FEATURE-LENGTH FILMS DIRECTED BY STEVEN SPIELBERG

Duel (Universal, 1972)

The Sugarland Express (Universal, 1974)

Jaws (Universal, 1975)

Close Encounters of the Third Kind (Columbia, 1977)

1941 (Columbia/Universal/A-Team, 1979)

Raiders of the Lost Ark (Paramount/Lucasfilm, 1981)

E.T.: The Extraterrestrial (Universal, 1982)

Twilight Zone – The Movie (Warner Brothers, 1983)

Indiana Jones and the Temple of Doom (Paramount/Lucasfilm, 1984)

The Color Purple (Warner Brothers/Amblin/Guber-Peters, 1985)

Empire of the Sun (Warner Brothers/Amblin, 1987)

Indiana Jones and the Last Crusade (Paramount/Lucasfilm, 1989)

Always (Universal/United Artists/Amblin, 1989)

Hook (Tristar/Amblin, 1991)

Jurassic Park (Universal/Amblin, 1993)

Schindler's List (Universal/Amblin, 1993)

Lost World: Jurassic Park (Universal/Amblin, 1997)

Amistad (DreamWorks SKG, 1998)

FEATURE-LENGTH FILMS WITH SPIELBERG AS EXECUTIVE PRODUCER

I Wanna Hold Your Hand (Universal, 1978)

Used Cars (Columbia, 1980)

Continental Divide (Universal, 1981)

Poltergeist (MGM, 1982)

Twilight Zone – the Movie (Warner Brothers, 1983)

Gremlins (Warner Brothers/Amblin, 1984)

Fandango (Warner Brothers/Amblin, 1985)

The Goonies (Warner Brothers/Amblin, 1985)

Back to the Future (Universal/Amblin, 1985)

Young Sherlock Holmes (Paramount/Amblin, 1985)

The Money Pit (Universal/Amblin, 1986)

An American Tail (Universal/Amblin, 1986)

Innerspace (Warner Brothers/Amblin/Guber-Peters, 1987)

Batteries not included (Universal/Amblin, 1987)

Harry and the Hendersons (Universal/Amblin, 1987)

Who Framed Roger Rabbit? (Touchstone/Amblin, 1988)

The Land Before Time (Universal/Amblin, 1988)

Back to the Future II (Universal/Amblin, 1989)

Dad (Universal/Amblin, 1989)

Back to the Future III (Universal/Amblin, 1990)

Gremlins II – The New Batch (Warner Brothers/Amblin, 1990)

Joe Versus the Volcano (Warner Brothers/Amblin, 1990)

Arachnophobia (Hollywood Pictures/Amblin, 1990)

An American Tail II –Fievel Goes West (Universal/Amblin, 1991)

Cape Fear (Universal/Amblin, 1991)

Noises Off (Touchstone/Amblin, 1992)

A Far-off Place (Touchstone/Amblin, 1993)

We're Back! A Dinosaur's Story (Universal/Amblin, 1993)

The Flintstones (Universal/Amblin, 1994)

Casper (Universal/Amblin, 1995)

The Little Rascals (Universal/King Features/Amblin, 1995)

How to Make an American Quilt (Universal/Amblin, 1995)

To Wong Foo, Thanks for Everything, Julie Newmar (Universal/Amblin, 1995)

The Bridges of Madison County (Warner Brothers/Amblin, 1995)

Balto (Universal/Amblin, 1996)

Twister (Universal/Warner Brothers/Amblin, 1996)

GLOSSARY

anti-Semitic targeting Jewish people as the object of insults or violence

box-office the front of the cinema where tickets are sold. It also describes the total amount of money earned through the sale of tickets for a film.

cast the actors who play the roles in a film

composition the way in which the director arranges the images that appear on the screen

continuity how scenes in a film follow naturally from one to another

custody the legal right to care for a child

director the person who supervises all aspects of how a film is made – acting, scenery, lighting and music – to make sure the film works as it is intended

esprit a lively intelligence

executive producer the person who is finally responsible for the business matters and production of several films, while each film also has its own producer

extraterrestrial coming from outside Earth, usually a creature who comes from outer space

feature-length long enough to be the main cinema feature

film rights the legal rights to adapt a play, novel or short story into a film.

focus the adjustment of a camera lens so that the objects being filmed appear clearly and are not blurred

footage a particular length of motion picture film, which is wound around reels and can be measured by the foot – it usually describes a sequence of a film

galley proofs pages supplied to an author or publisher in order to check for mistakes before a book is printed

Hollywood a district in Los Angeles, California, which is the centre of the American film business. Hollywood can also be used as a general term to describe commercial American films.

Holocaust the systematic slaughter of millions of Jews in Nazi camps during the Second World War (1939–1945).

ingenuity intelligence with inventiveness

location a place where a film is being shot outside rather than inside a studio

mainstream appealing to a wide range of audiences by being easy to understand and by avoiding any offence

manslaughter the unintentional killing of another human being

negative the original film obtained from the camera when filming was done

Oscar (also known as an Academy Award) one of a group of statuettes awarded annually by the American Academy of Motion Picture Arts and Sciences for professional achievement in motion pictures

persecution causing harm to a group because of its beliefs, race or religion

prequel an invented word (using 'sequel' as its root) to describe a story that concerns events that occurred before the action that takes place in another story

prodigious large size or amount

producer the person who is responsible for raising money for a film as well as employing the crew that will work on it. It is up to the producer to ensure that the film does not fall behind schedule and that it is delivered on time.

promote advertise and generally make sure that a film receives a great deal of publicity in order to attract large audiences to it

revolt rise up against a power or government

screenplay a film or television script that describes the plot of a story and includes instructions for the film-making team

sequel a follow-up to a successful story or film, retaining many of the characters from the first story

serial a cinema, radio or television programme that appears regularly, usually each week

soundtrack the sound and music that is recorded to accompany the visual images of a film

special effects unusual visual or sound effects that cannot be produced through normal filming. Special effects artists use computers, enlarged photographic images, models and other devices to simulate natural disasters and science fiction sequences.

studio a room that is specially equipped for making a film or other recording, or the buildings and land that a company needs to make films

suburb/an concerning a small residential community outside a city or town

synagogue a Jewish place of worship

trilogy a series of three related books, plays or films

INDEX